In Defense of the Marfa Lights

Other Books by James Bunnell

Seeing Marfa Lights

Night Orbs

Hunting Marfa Lights

Strange Lights in West Texas

In Defense of the Marfa Lights

James Bunnell

ISBN: 978-1-09837-144-9

Lacey Publishing Company

Benbrook, Texas

Table of Contents

In Defense of the Marfa Lights

Forward

Reports of mysterious lights - lights of unknown origin – come from many locations on this earth, including the ranchland east of Marfa, a small West Texas town in the United States. Here, in fact, "The Marfa Lights" are so well known that the state of Texas created a roadside park for the many curious travelers and locals who stand at night looking across a wide expanse of ranchland (Mitchell Flat) with the hope of seeing them. Some visitors declare distant, moving lights to be "mysterious," while more skeptical visitors may tell you that what they saw were ranch lights and vehicle headlights. Who is right? There have been countless magazine articles, newspaper accounts, books, and television programs that raise the question but never quite answer it. A team of scientists, state of the art equipment, and time (years) might do it. But at this point in time, the "answer" boils down to a choice between two camps. There are the light gazers who, based on onsite experience or on what they have read, feel strongly that unusual light activity does exist on this expanse of ranchland. And then there are those who are equally convinced that all the lights in Mitchell Flat will prove to be as readily explainable as light from known sources.

I am in the "mysterious lights do exist camp." I call them "MLs" for short. I believe it is fair to say that I have spent more time, effort, and money actively researching this fascinating West Texas light phenomena than anyone else. It was initially meant to be a short study at the start of my retirement from aerospace engineering. It turned out to be a years-long project, working as a one-man team (with the help of one very patient woman). I collected ten years of firsthand observations, photographs of many hundreds of lights, and compiled a unique base of my own photographic evidence. Based on that experience, I have concluded that some of the lights located east of Marfa, Texas are indeed mysterious, and are natural phenomena that deserve scientific study. My **Strange Lights in West Texas** book,

(Bunnell, 2015), as well as my website, www.marfatxlights.com, and two previous books provide support for this conclusion.

Several independent investigators have worked hard to support the idea that any nocturnal light in Mitchell Flat can be easily explained when sufficient evidence is available. **Mysteries of the Marfa Lights Revealed** (Wagers & Wagers, 2013) and **The Marfa Lights, Examining the Photographic Evidence** (Aymerich & Olmos, 2020) are two published books that attempt to make the case for explainable events.

I have no quarrel with the Wagers (2013) book. It is a scholarly work that focuses on a number of observations made by individuals who may have seen odd-looking lights and assumed them to be mysterious when they were instead explainable lights. To their credit, the Wagers did travel to Marfa, visited the Marfa Lights View Park (MLVP), and looked for the lights. Unfortunately, they failed to see them. But that failure is not surprising: Seeing MLs in action requires either great luck or extreme patience.

During the first five years of my research (2000 through 2004), I was able to catalog only 12 MLs. I averaged 60-70 days a year standing in Mitchell Flat with my mobile cameras. My onsite ML searches were, over the years, augmented by a total of 10 automated night cameras that recorded video every night. Three very interested Mitchell Flat ranchers (including one from the Mitchell family) made this possible by giving me input, encouragement, and access to what became my camera stations. My first automated station, "Roofus," was in operation by 2003 with one camera, and a second station, "Snoopy," was added in 2004 (also with one camera until a second was added in 2008). Starting in 2006, my success rate with finding MLs improved significantly when I was given access to a more central location in Mitchell Flat for two additional monitoring stations, "Owlbert" A & B. This gave me seven more night-cameras. By then, I also had the benefit of accumulated experience. Even so, over ten years (2000-2009), I was able to document only 54 mysterious lights.

Given these results, it is not difficult to understand how even new, enthusiastic researchers might spend many nights observing and still conclude (mistakenly) that there is nothing to see but vehicle lights. Like the phenomena of ball lightning, their infrequent appearances make research into MLs time consuming, difficult, and expensive. It is only after years of relentless effort, and because I have seen a large number of lights, but a much smaller number of MLs, that I can say with confidence that intriguing, scientifically unexplained lights do exist near Marfa and, by extension, are likely to occur in other places around the world.

In contrast to the Wagers' book, I do take strong exception to the work of Aymerich and Olmos. Their methods and results seriously mislead readers. They worked solely in Spain, using computer software (Google Earth) and my copyrighted photographs (with absolutely no permission to publish). They apparently saw no need for "boots on the ground," and they had a strong monetary incentive to design elaborate alternate explanations. Their book (for sale in Europe for 32 Euros) is part of their long-running UFO "debunking business."

This short response to their more elaborate 174-page production will, I hope, cause readers to have second thoughts before accepting conclusions based on a computer-driven "from-a-distance research project" into these naturally occurring, rare events. This is my side of the story. For readers who are just discovering the Marfa Lights, I hope what follows here will serve as a compact introduction to one of Earth's intriguing, unsolved mysteries.

Part 1

Demise of the Marfa Lights has been greatly exaggerated…

In the summer of 2020, Manuel Aymerich and V.J. Ballester Olmos published an article on the internet and are now selling a book version in Europe titled ***The Marfa Lights / Examining the Photographic Evidence (2003-2007)***. The authors have published, without my permission, copyrighted pictures from my websites and two of my books with the intent of "proving" that the Marfa Lights do not exist. Using the Google Earth app and photographic **"overlay"** software, they have produced an overwhelming number of calculations and graphs. and, from a distance, their work appears impressive. If you read more thoroughly, however, you will see (through all the "if's, and's, and but's") that it is a mighty and strained effort to push forward a "Vehicle Headlights (**VHL**) Theory." If their readers accept that theory, they are accepting a multitude of assumptions that Aymerich and Olmos have chosen to make in order to get the outcomes they want (i.e., put lights on roads). That doesn't sound much like a scientific endeavor, does it? It's not. It's two UFO debunkers writing for profit.

At the outset, you should also know that fourteen photographs from my ***Strange Lights in West Texas*** book appear 52 times across 36 figures in the Aymerich/Olmos work, all published without my permission. In addition, they have used several photographs from my websites and two other books. These two fellows skipped over most of my books, but they absolutely ignored the statement on page 2: "**All rights reserved. No part of this book may be reproduced or transmitted in any form or by any means, electronic or mechanical, including photocopying, recording or by any informational storage and retrieval system, without written permission from the author, except for the inclusion of brief quotations in a review.**" [**Night Orbs**, Copyright 2003: ISBN 0-9709249-2-5; **Hunting Marfa Lights**, Copyright 2009: ISBN 13:9780970924940; and **Strange Lights in West Texas,** Copyright 2015: ISBN 978-0-9709249-7-1].

Although their title implies it, these authors did not do a 4-year study; they used photographs and data from my 10-year, actual, on-site study, and ran the numbers (theirs), to produce new outcomes. This is not a report of my work. It is a reworking of my work and it is not research. I strongly disagree both with their "findings" and with their ethics.

Manuel Borraz Aymerich and Vicente J. Olmos reside in Spain; neither have been to Marfa, Texas. Instead, they have relied (heavily) on Google Earth to take them there. Although not scientists, they have made reputations in the EU as UFO "debunkers." Mr. Olmos calls himself a "citizen scientist." He began contacting me about 5 years ago asking for information on my Marfa Lights project. When I learned that we had a mutual friend, an Italian physicist who has worked on the Hessdalen Lights project (a government/university funded project investigating similar earth-light phenomena in Norway) as well as other Earth Light locations in Italy and South America, I began responding to his questions, including details of my photographic data. While this information was shared in the interest of research, I never authorized reproduction of my copyrighted data or photographs. I was saddened and angered to see that these two people have lifted slices of my work to build a pseudo-research study that I believe is simply intended to replace my findings with theirs.

It is, of course, not uncommon for individuals to reach dissimilar conclusions about data sets, especially when reviewing investigative material considered to be mysterious or unexplained. I would have welcomed any honest and factual review of my work, and I initially believed that was the purpose of Olmos' inquiries. Now looking back, I do not think this was an honest and factual review. I think it was meant to shut down further inquiry into the Marfa Lights. And that thought troubles me equally as much as their profiting from a book that is based almost wholly on my work.

Since several members of the scientific community have praised this work by Aymerich/Olmos, I want to briefly discuss, in a few short paragraphs here, some basic and important issues with respect to the Marfa Lights. Following this, I examine (in Part 2) five examples of mysterious lights that have been "reworked" by Aymerich/ Olmos and explain my own take on what they have done. In closing, I provide (in Part 3) a photographic summary of my camera sites and field equipment.

I well understand that your time is precious. I sincerely hope that, before you render judgement on the nature of the Marfa Lights phenomena, you will find the time to consider **these** *issues.*

The role of roads

Aymerich and Olmos have never traveled to Marfa, Texas, nor have they traveled roads in the high desert land surrounding Marfa. That's important. There are many ranch roads in Mitchell Flat (this is the area where mysterious lights were first reported by settlers and Native Americans (Brueske, 1988) in the 19th century. **If you have not driven a vehicle on this ranchland, you may be unaware of the fact that none of these roads are paved and most are simply dirt trails**. **If a light on Mitchell Flat looks or moves in a way not typical of a truck or a car** (e.g., moving too fast for the terrain, flying above ground and fence lines, not stopping at locked gates), **that light may actually not be from a truck or a car.**

If a light follows a known road, and looks like usual traffic on that road, is it a vehicle headlight? Most probably it is. If a light appears in an area far from a road, is it a vehicle headlight? Maybe yes, maybe no. In Mitchell Flat, *a light that crosses a road, or is near a road, is not necessarily a VHL* (Vehicle Head Light). Conversely, *a light that appears far from a road is not necessarily an ML* (Mysterious Light). Location is a major factor in describing a light that appears suddenly in the distance and the darkness of night, but it is far from being the only factor. Is it flying? Fast-moving? Constant "on," or "on-off"? What route does it take from start to end? What is its physical appearance? What atmospheric conditions are in play? What other "behavioral" characteristics does it exhibit?

There are dirt roads and trails throughout Mitchell Flat and on the mesas to the south, but only the Nopal to Escondido Ranch road and the 101 Ranch Road are county maintained and equipped with cattle guards, permitting relatively fast travel at speeds with potential to be mistaken for mysterious lights. In my experience, MLs were originating near fault lines in the southeast part of Mitchell Flat and tended to travel to the Northwest until they exhausted energy and extinguished. None of the MLs that I identified ever came close to being aligned with the 101 Ranch Road. Vehicle traffic on Nopal Road has the greatest potential for misidentification. It is a dirt road, and although maintained by the county, there are many unexpected hindrances, such as sleeping cows, deep water after rains, holes, turns, raised cattle guards and closed gates. Importantly, **VHLs driving on Nopal had to stop at the Barlight locked gate, something no ML ever did**.

Google Earth, like so many of our digital tools, can give us a wealth of information. But in this instance particularly, to substitute an app for eyes, judgement, and experience is beyond naive. That resource, the human factor, is sorely missing in the Aymerich/Olmos approach.

Magnetic versus "true north" vectors

The most frequently cited issue Aymerich/Olmos took with my work has to do with my published magnetic bearings from the **Marfa Lights View Park** (**MLVP; MLVC** in the Aymerich/Olmos version). They provide graphs and tables revealing magnetic errors as much as four degrees when converted to the true north vectors they obtained using Google Earth. Based on this finding, they concluded that I did not know where the lights I photographed were located. They took that conclusion as an open invitation to make significant lateral location adjustments, as needed, to find ranch roads (or dirt trails) that "could have been" where ranch vehicles were moving with headlights ablaze. Thus, MLs become VHLs.

12

What was the nature of these magnetic errors and how did they impact the mysterious lights I photographed? "**True north**" vectors, of course, are measured with respect to the (global) North Pole and are independent from local conditions. **Magnetic vectors**, in contrast, are measured with respect to a gradually changing (also global) magnetic north **and can be locally influenced by electrical and metallic factors**. Aymerich/Olmos attributed magnetic vector errors to metal in the structured viewing platform of the MLVP. I contributed to that presumption by explaining to Olmos that, during my initial years of research (2003-2004), I did my observing from the Southwest Plaque, located 52 meters from the center of the viewing platform. At that time, I did this to minimize the possible magnetic influence of the MLVP structure. My thinking changed as I reviewed my field notes and **discovered that magnetic vectors from the same vantage points were different from year to year.**

Today I would say that magnetic vectors vary throughout the Mitchell Flat region (where MLs have been reported) due to ever-changing electric fields beneath that area. Reviewing data from different years for both MLVP and non-MLVP mobile camera locations (i.e., near Snoopy and Owlbert/Barlight), I can see significant magnetic vector changes over time. Geology tells us that the Marfa Basin resulted from collision of two earth platelets. The Marathon Uplift is riding over the Diablo Platform to create, beneath Mitchell Flat, a collision of massive igneous rocks (McGookey, 2004). NASA Scientist Dr. Friedemann T. Freund has shown with laboratory experiments that igneous rock, when subjected to extreme stress, behaves like a large battery (Freund, 2006). In the case of Mitchell Flat, underground electrical potential is likely to be extraordinarily high and ever changing because the region is heavily bombarded by lightning strikes in stormy seasons. For example, on the night of June 3, 2005, a series of intense thunderstorms pumped thousands of cloud-to-ground lightning strikes into the region (Stephan, Bunnell, Klier, Komala-Noor, 2011).

Figure 1a: The 1st of three intense lightning strike photos on 6-3-2005,

Figure 1b: The 2nd of three intense lightning strike photos on 6-3-2005.

14

Figure 1c. The 3rd of three intense lightning strike photos on 6-3-2005 sending electricity (8,000 lightning strikes) into Mitchell Flat in about 20 minutes near where MLs usually originate.

I suspect that these circumstances, along with seismic stress, are likely the source of changing electrical fields, and associated magnetic fields, beneath Mitchell Flat. Moreover, I suspect that **these subsurface electrical fields may be the very reason MLs do appear from time to time in Mitchell Flat** (see **Strange Lights**, Chapter 7). It is no coincidence, I think, that most MLs originate near existing fault lines and fly to the northwest roughly parallel to fault lines as shown in the Part 2, Example 5.

Magnetic vectors are convenient to use in the field because we can take vector measurements anywhere with a compass. Most visitors to the MLVP have compass apps in their cell phones. When observing from the View Park, I used compass-equipped binoculars to obtain magnetic vectors to ML beginning and ending points. In my books, I also published directional information for background terrain so that my readers/visitors to the MLVP could look for MLs in the general directions where my camera had found them, and thereby avoid looking at car lights on Highway 67. My magnetic vectors served that purpose; converting to "true north" would not have changed the terrain view and would have been useless directional information to a visitor at the MLVP.

That said, it is important to understand that ML route development – that is, calculating the path the ML took from first appearance to final disappearance -- <u>was accomplished using night camera video data.</u> Magnetic directional data was used only to help establish beginning and ending points. Possible beginning and ending errors, to whatever extent they may have existed, were not a critical factor in evaluating ML routes relative to road systems in Mitchell Flat. Because of fence lines and terrain obstacles, vehicle non-road travel for any distance at flight speeds of MLs was simply not possible. In most cases, MLs originated in the SE and traveled NW. **Unidentified lights traveling NW, to be VHLs, <u>had to be aligned</u> with Nopal Road to achieve ML travel speeds, and, if on Nopal, had to show a 4-to-6-minute stop-go-stop-go pattern at the Barlight locked gate**.

I was able to determine light trajectories because my night cameras accurately recorded light route vectors as a function of elapsed time with respect to Barlight's Central Mercury Vapor Lamp (CMV). ML routes rarely progressed in straight lines in their northwest journeys. They flew cross country, above fence lines. **<u>Their trajectories typically zigzagged or curved and did not mirror roads in Mitchell Flat</u>**. Part 2, Example 1, provides an explanation of route development for ML2b, May 8, 2003, as shown in **Strange Lights**, Map 7. The same techniques were also used to develop ML routes presented in Maps 6, 8, and 10 of that book. None of these routes correspond to available roads.

Looming and mirage conditions?

Aymerich/Olmos brought to ground the MLs that I found to be above ground and flying high in the air, attributing their "apparent" altitude to mirages or atmospheric looming. Perhaps they presumed that, being an engineer, I would not have knowledge of mirage conditions, even though I devoted Chapter 8 of **Strange Lights** to explaining those conditions and the role they play as a source of mistaken ML stories. For them, my airborne MLs were nothing more than atmospheric tricks plus any nearby ranch road/trail deemed sufficient for VHLs. **Since Google Earth has no capability to assess height of flying lights, it was possibly their best fallback position when vectors did not yield the story they wanted**. See Part 2, Example 2.

What was shaking my cameras? Nothing.

My 05/08/2003 exploding ML, along with other atypical MLs, are explained away as "camera shake," "camera movement," or "lens defects." However, my photograph of this particular ML clearly shows individual descending remnants following the explosion (see Example 2 in Part 2), inconsistent with their claim of camera shake. This is an excuse Aymerich/Olmos use multiple times to explain away photographic features inconsistent with their claim of VHLs.

My tripod (mobile) cameras changed over the years from film cameras to digital cameras. I used heavy duty tripods with weights as needed to counter wind gusts. On stormy nights, I packed up and left. Camera shake was not an issue. Nor was it an issue with my automated cameras. I was very much aware of how my cameras were faring in the wind and took care to not disturb them during video filming.

What I did/ what they did

Without automated night cameras, my study would not have been possible. These cameras were designed to photograph and save video images of 30 to 50 nights of data to onsite removable hard drives. I collected and replaced the drives monthly and reviewed the data in my home office (500 miles from Marfa). I tagged as ULs (Unknown Lights) any unusual, "suspect" lights that I had photographed onsite with my tripod cameras. These ULs remained in that status until I completed a thorough review of the automated night camera data. Based on careful consideration of all data sources, they would then be identified as vehicle headlights (VHLs), or mysterious lights (MLs), or would remain ULs pending additional data that would permit a more definitive identification. ***Upgrading a UL to ML status involved careful review of all data sources including night camera data, onsite observations and tripod photography, a review of field notes, and route development.*** Initially, I also tracked earth and solar (coronal mass ejections) weather data but discontinued that effort after finding no significant correlations with ML appearances.

The importance of what actually happened. Although my night and mobile cameras provided powerful photographic data that allowed me to document and analyze these unusual lights in Mitchell Flat, I should underscore the fact that eliminating VHLs was, in fact, easy to do. MLs were originating mostly to the southeast, so that was a prime direction to monitor. When a light did appear, I noted if it came from and/or went to a ranch house or work area. Was it moving at a speed possible only on Nopal Road? Faster than possible? Was it on Nopal Road? The locked gate and S-turn on that road were, of course, excellent indicators of vehicles on Nopal. But there were other clues: Did the light source show red taillights when crossing bumpy cattle guards and slowing to cross mud holes? If the light was not on Nopal, how fast was it going? Did it stop at fence lines? Did the light bounce up and down as a vehicle might do on rough terrain? Did the light show a beam? Seen from the side or at an angle, headlight beams are usually apparent. This was the case for traffic on Nopal Road when viewed

18

from the MLVP. There were also rare occasions when I observed powerful hand-held lights, and even flashlights (paired with too much beer, and/or a twisted sense of humor). All of those light sources were easy to identify, especially the hand-held variety.

Aymerich/Olmos would have you think that I was photographing VHLs without a clue. That reflects their lack of understanding about what I did as well as their total and important lack of experience with the actual terrain in Mitchell Flat.

My reading of what the Aymerich/ Olmos team did was (1) contact me and obtain as much information and data as possible from 3 books, my websites, and 10+ years of my investigative work; (2) comb through the data for cases (primarily my earliest data) that would yield to a reworking through Google Earth, and (3) using Google Earth not only to find errors in my work (I'm sure there are some), but to make assumptions about what the "corrections" should be. With their assumption-based corrections in place, they produced seemingly plausible cases for concluding: Hey! no mystery here.... just headlights! If you look at their work with that in mind, the "noise" in their approach becomes very apparent. **It appears, for example, that any light I found to be flying could not have been found flying by their system.** As I mentioned previously in connection with the looming issue, since they are quite certain that the lights are on roads, and they have no resource other than Google Earth, anything I perceived as flying would instead be the result of atmospheric refraction (mirage, looming). **"Google Earth imagery does not consider atmospheric refraction"** (Aymerich & Olmos, p.130). Therefore, they reason, **"Since our main goal has been to verify or refute the alleged mysterious nature of the photographed lights, no attempt has been made to estimate the exact magnitude of the existing refraction..." (p.131)**. *Nothing will be flying for them!* For those of you who wish to validate some of their work, note how often they find "errors" in my work and then, amazingly, are able, with Google Earth, **to use my "flawed" data to correct my work and put those lights on roads, <u>relocating them by as much as ten kilometers,</u>**

when necessary. Here is an example (page 90 in the Aymerich/Olmos version):

> "As in other cases studied above, the given position of the start of ML3 does not correspond with the azimuth of the same spot obtained with the help of Google Earth…Again, this is a clear indication of <u>calculations based on wrong data that would prevent assigning the route followed by the light to any recognized terrain path</u>. As we will show graphically later, there are factual differences in the locations estimated by Bunnell." [Their full strained 'analysis' takes 14 pages.]

They are saying (I think) two things: (1) my data collection and calculations are wrong, and (2) my calculations do not indicate that this ML was on a road. I absolutely <u>do not</u> believe that my data and calculations are wrong, but they are correct on the second point: the light was in the air above, and the terrain below it was not a road. I find it incredible that these fellows can fix so much with Google Earth.

I did wonder, as I looked over their numerous forays through my photos and data, just how many updates the Google Earth software had been through since it first became public in 2005. In Example #4 of Part 2, Aymerich/ Olmos discuss a vehicle possibly being on what they call a "detour" from a mesa road. Were they able to read this road "detour" sign using Google Earth satellite data from 2018 or 2019? Was it there 14-15 years earlier, in 2004, when this ML appeared? Do they expect us to believe that Google Earth terrain (which is satellite data) would show a readable 2004 detour sign, on this mesa road? **Although I traveled this mesa several times in those early years, I don't know if that road even existed then. But I do know that lengthy backing up is less likely than simply doing a U-turn through the brush for some rancher driving a large, four-wheel-drive truck.** Please read the quoted passage in Part 2, Example 4, to understand how difficult it was for them to choose a road. It is quite amazing to see something like that, even from a pseudo-scientific paper.

Rare as earthquakes in West Texas

MLs appear rarely and at unpredictable times. This is the biggest obstacle to investigating this phenomenon. While there are lights in Mitchell Flat every night, most of them are vehicle and aircraft lights; ML appearances are extremely **infrequent**. This issue was compounded by the fact that I was onsite, on average, for 6-12 days, 9 to 11 times per year. Although I have not tabulated the exact number of days I spent hunting lights in Mitchell Flat, my estimate puts the total at about 750 days (400 in the first five years and 350 in the second). Over the span of my 10-year effort I found 54 light events that I considered unusual enough to include in my data set of MLs. With multiple events on some nights, it is amazing to me that these lights appeared in front of my cameras for only 38 nights of the 10 years that I spent looking for them. Often, I had to wait multiple months before being rewarded with the next ML event. These phenomena, during the time of my investigation, were rare. For a person in Spain to sit in front of a computer screen, "looking" at Mitchell Flat via US government "Google Earth" satellite data -- pictures of terrain taken 10-15 years beyond the time of my work -- and declaring that I was being easily fooled by vehicle lights is disappointing; actually, laughable.

The extreme infrequency of MLs makes studying earth light phenomena quite challenging, but not impossible. Ball lightning is another infrequently observed event that now is at least partially recognized as a legitimate phenomenon; it too has shown unexplained abilities to travel horizontally not only through the air, but, by some reports, even through doors or closed windows. My photographs and route tracking data show that MLs, like ball lightning, may also have unexpected abilities to travel, including into the wind. The possibility of that is significant; an important reason for scientific investigation (see Chapter 9 of Strange Lights).

Although the biggest hinderance to ML investigation is the infrequency of their appearance, it is also important to recognize that the chance of finding any ML using Google Earth is absolute zero.

Aymerich / Olmos had zero chance of finding MLs, just as they had zero chance of finding a vehicle behind the lights I photographed. There are many statements in their book that indicate a bias for vehicle-based explanations, but no mentions of photographs that show vehicles hanging tenaciously attached to my lights. Their ability to overlay my photographs of MLs onto photographs of Google Earth roads does not prove that I was photographing vehicle headlights. It certainly doesn't prove that MLs don't exist. Why?

First, consider that neither they nor I, nor anyone to date, has tackled this issue with the time and scientific resources (camera power and human eyes and hours) that would be needed for a definitive answer. Second, and most critical here, Aymerich/ Olmos started with the biased assumption that all of these lights were vehicle headlights.

They started with the premise: if we can design a logical narrative and put it on or near a road, that proves it's a vehicle. **I have no trouble with concluding this, given the extraordinary contortions they went through to justify their product. I have attempted to give you a taste of that with the Part 2 examples in this book. With countless re-figuring of vectors and new pathways, and narratives molded to fit (all providing a heightened sense of validity), they want readers to believe that what they have produced is a valid scientific analysis, a piece of research that "proves" the Marfa Lights exist only on the front end of vehicles. <u>What they have actually proved is that they can create a narrative that supports that idea.</u> And much like narratives of historical fiction, produced by individuals with agendas, the conclusions their audience comes away with may be miles away from what that piece of history, if it could be truly known, would tell.**

I am now retired from active investigation of the Marfa Lights, but I hate to see these phenomena, and, by association, worldwide research of "Earth Lights," cut asunder because two people do "debunking" for a living. It is my opinion that this is a grossly misplaced and unfortunate effort to snuff out future scientific investigation of unexplained lights based on this remote, computer-driven effort to explain them as man-made light sources. With their work, Aymerich and Olmos have buried real images and real events beneath a deep swamp of moveable degrees, graphs, and claims based on their own assumptions, all of which are deliberately designed, I think, to discourage close examination. Few scientists would have the time and interest to study, judge their assumptions and conclusions, and validate what has been done here, especially when validation would only apply to their narrative, not to the study of the actual phenomena in question. I think Aymerich/Olmos are very much aware of that.

In Part 2 to this response, I briefly discuss five examples of ML cases to explain why I think these two people did not get it right. My strategy was much different from theirs. I defend my work because I have seen, experienced, and photographed enough in Mitchell Flat to know that unusual light phenomena do indeed appear in that area. I cannot say my own work is without errors. What I can say is that my work stands much closer than theirs to reality, and, I hope, to the truth.

At this point, we can only speculate as to the true nature of MLs. Finding answers will be for a younger generation of scientists. For success, they will need to be equipped with a dedicated team and technological equipment that includes more than Google Earth. At the very least, they will need high resolution infrared video cameras that capture spectra, plus an intense curiosity about lights in the distance, in the dark, that do not come with fenders and taillights. They will also need an abundance of patience.

PART 2

Five Detailed Examples

| Example #1 | ML2b route development May 8, 2003 |

Aymerich/Olmos insist that my magnetic bearings were seriously flawed and thereby justify their making significant lateral position adjustments. To dispute that, I provide the following example showing the **development of the path of ML2b** (May 8, 2003) using data **from my tripod camera** at the MLVP, **the Roofus night camera,** and **the "central mercury vapor light" (CMV)**. Figure 2, shown here, provides route information for this example and location information for key features in Mitchell Flat (Map 7, **Strange Lights**, pp. 90-94). **Note: the solid, zigzagging red line on map is the path of ML2b.**

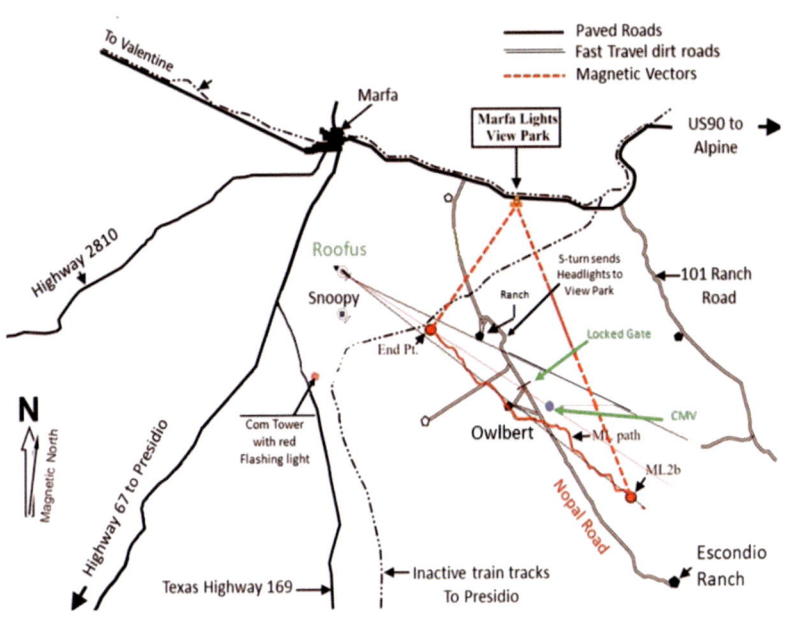

Figure 2. *Route development for ML2b (5/8/2003) using Roofus video data and the CMV (Central Mercury Vapor light, a known stationary point), with pertinent reference coordinates below:*

My location that night at SW Plaque in MLVP: N30deg 16.497min
W103deg 53.067min

Roofus location: N30deg 13.316min
W104deg 00.118 min

CMV location: N30deg 08.256min
W103deg 51.774min

Locked Gate: N30deg 9.453min
W103deg 52.727min

ML2b start point (approx. location) N30deg 5.65min
W103deg 48.5min

ML2b exhausts & goes out (approx. location) N30deg 11.8min
W103deg 57.3min

The Path: ML2b started in the southeast part of Mitchell Flat east of Nopal Road (see above map) and flew to the northwest. It crossed Nopal Road southeast of the **locked gate** and continued NW without stopping until exhausting energy and going out near the old railroad tracks to Presidio. This ML path is a typical off-road, zigzag trek that crosses Nopal Road as well as multiple fence lines, possible only because it was flying above them. It was not on Nopal Road; it crossed in the air above it. It did not start at a ranch house or go to a ranch house. Instead, it started east of Nopal and ended near inactive railroad tracks west of Nopal. Notice the zigzag path it followed. This path was captured by Roofus, my only night camera in May, 2003.

The Data: I was standing beside my camera at the Marfa Lights View Park (see Fig.2, MLVP coordinates) and searching the terrain when this unknown light appeared. I mentally recorded the initial magnetic bearing (vector) for this light and immediately began locating it in my camera. As soon as the target light was acquired, I entered the starting vector in my field notebook. **My tripod field camera photographs captured information that was important to establishing beginning and ending locations (see Fig.2, coordinates) with respect to terrain, regardless of how we choose to describe those locations, i.e., via magnetic values (relation to magnetic north) or as true values (relation to the North Pole; true north).** My tripod camera provided a night view of the terrain as it appeared when viewed from the Marfa Lights View Park (MLVP); this was only one piece of the information needed to compute initial beginning and ending locations for this light.

Roofus, my automatic night video camera (see Fig.2, coordinates), also caught this light and terrain, but from a very different angle and also provided beginning and ending information from a different perspective. Most importantly, however, this night video camera, mounted atop a ranch house and aimed in a constant view, continuously recorded both images of the distant moving light and its changing positions relative to the central mercury vapor light (CMV).

At this time, the CMV was an illuminated point in a fixed location on Barlight Ranch in Mitchell Flat.

With photographs from two cameras, one mobile and one stationary, and the fixed-point image (CMV) captured in tandem with a suspect light, it was possible to **derive movement by calculating incremental, angular displacements** between the suspect light and the Barlight CMV. This process was done by visual inspection of still video images using a template calibrated for measuring Roofus' stationary view of the moving light. Strange Lights (Map 7) graphically shows the zigzag route followed by ML2b. The Central Mercury Vapor (CMV) light was located at a bearing of 125.02 degrees from Roofus. **I used this fixed bearing <u>of the CMV in relation to the Roofus camera</u>, 125.02 degrees, as a reference point, making it possible to track ML2b progress as it flew to the Northwest. This is summarized in Table1 below.** The first (left) column in the table is elapsed flight time based on the Roofus clock. Roofus automatically ran every night; it detected ML2b as soon as it appeared. Elapsed time in Table 1 below is **minutes: seconds from first appearance**. From the point of origin, Roofus was continuously recording both the moving ML and the stationary CMV. The angular separation between the ML and the CMV at start was 1.69 degrees. The third column in the table below is the sum of the CMV location (125.02 degrees) and the advancing ML location (1.69 degrees to the right) = 126.71 degrees

Table 1. Data used to plot the route of ML2b, 5/8/2003.

Roofus: Elapsed Time	CMV To Roofus Vector (Constant)	Add-on Angle Between ML & CMV	Roofus to ML Changing Vector (Col.3 +125.02)	Notes
min:sec	degrees	degrees	degrees	
0:00	125.02	1.69	126.71	
0:39	.	1.64	126.66	
2:12	.	1.42	126.44	
2:39	.	1.39	126.41	
4:54	.	1.39	126.41	
5:25	.	1.39	126.41	
6:05	.	1.08	126.1	ML crosses Nopal Road
6:22	.	1.04	126.06	south of the Locked Gate.
6:41	.	1	126.02	
6:54	.	0.96	125.98	There were no matching
7:51	.	0.77	125.79	roads below the ML.
8:16	.	0.65	125.67	
8:22	.	0.62	125.64	Speed of flight
8:33	.	0.58	125.6	~56 mph = 90 km/hr
9:49	.	0.19	125.21	
9:55	.	0.15	125.17	
10:02	.	0.15	125.17	
10:03	.	0.12	125.14	
10:14	.	0.08	125.1	
10:34	.	0.04	125.06	
10:41	.	0.02	125.04	
10:55	.	0	125.02	CMV/ML/Roofus aligned.
10:58	.	-0.05	124.97	
11:02	.	-0.07	124.95	ML now moving left
11:06	.	-0.08	124.94	of CMV.
11:09	.	-0.12	124.9	
11:14	.	-0.12	124.9	
11:38	.	-0.28	124.74	
11:55	.	-0.39	124.63	
12:10	.	-0.5	124.52	
12:29	.	-0.62	124.4	
12:40	.	-0.69	124.33	
12:51	.	-0.77	124.25	ML exhausts
13:39	.	-0.77	124.25	near railroad tracks.
13:57	125.02	-0.77	124.25	

(the compass direction of the ML as viewed by Roofus). Thirty-nine seconds later, the space between the moving ML and the fixed CMV was reduced to 1.64 degrees. As the data recording continues, the gap between the ML and the CMV continues to be reduced as a result of

ML advancement. At flight time 10 minutes and 55 seconds, the ML and CMV lights merge (as viewed from Roofus). Following that the ML emerges on the left side of the CMV light as it continues its journey until exhausting energy and going out near the railroad tracks.

Availability of this data made it possible to trace the path followed by this ML as it flew from an initial location southeast of the MLVP to its final point of exhaustion near the old Presidio railroad tracks. As Figure 2 above shows, this ML crossed Nopal Road before reaching the locked gate and expired near the railroad tracks west of Nopal Road. It was not a vehicle!

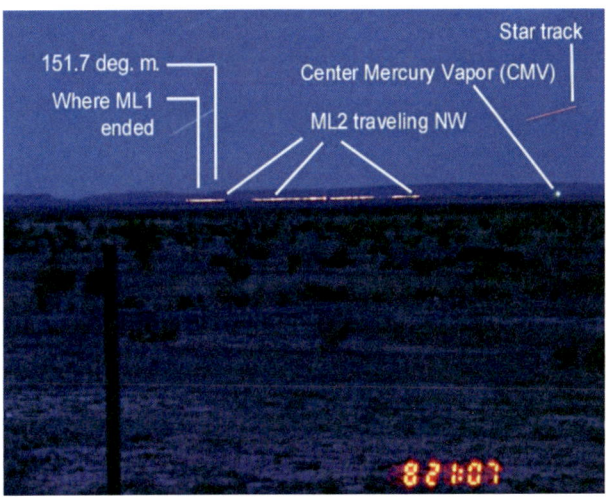

Figure 3. This photograph (Fig. 30; Strange Lights), taken from the MLVP, shows the first minutes of ML2b flying NW. At this point, the CMV is visible on the right side of the image.

The Problem: **Aymerich/Olmos claim this ML was a vehicle driving on Nopal Road** (Aymerich/Olmos, ~pp.58-87). **They devoted 29 pages, including 26 figures, six graphs and one table of their book** (a snowstorm of details) in an extraordinary and strained effort to convince their readers that this was a VHL driving NW on Nopal Road. The route zigzagged from decidedly east of Nopal Road to well west of Nopal Road, as shown in Figure 2 above. ML2b crossed Nopal Road before reaching the locked gate; it was not a VHL driving on Nopal Road. **Aymerich/Olmos are wrong <u>for following reasons:</u>**

(1) They base part of their argument on my use of "magnetic vectors," claiming that using this unit of measure makes my analyzed trajectory wrong. **I assert that the issue of using "true north" versus magnetic vectors, and possible errors in declination (difference of magnetic from true north) are irrelevant. The angle between beginning and ending points is correct regardless of possible declination errors because converting to true values moves both points equally in the same direction.** To plot the beginning and end points, I used the published declination of +7.3 degrees. [Aymerich/Olmos claim that declination varied over time by as much as 4.3 degrees beyond the published number (a magnitude I doubt). I do agree that it probably varied, but by smaller magnitude and affected the entire area rather than just the MLVP, as I mentioned in Part 1.] Also important is the fact that my MLVP magnetic vectors figure into this equation only at beginning and end points; my route analysis is based on two known, stationary points (Roofus & CMV) as a function of elapsed time. Thanks to Roofus data and the CMV stationary reference, route analysis clearly shows that this ML was <u>not</u> **a vehicle traveling** on Nopal Road.

(2) Roofus, with a clear view of both the advancing ML and its changing positions relative to the CMV, enabled an accurate tracking of the ML route that does not align with Nopal Road and would not align even if questionable declination adjustments were applied to beginning and end points. Roofus data, in relation to time and the CMV, support that conclusion. To recap, Map 7 in **Strange Lights**, shows this light starting well east of Nopal and following a non-stop, zigzag path to the northwest. **To do this, it had to be in the air, flying above fence lines**.

(3) Most notably, **this ML flew northwest without stopping at the locked gate on Nopal Road**, something a vehicle would not be able to do. Stopping at that gate was an unavoidable requirement for anyone traveling to Barlight Ranch from the Marfa/Alpine Highway or

passing Barlight in either direction, from the southeast or northwest toward the highway. This was a convenient way to identify a vehicle on Nopal, because opening the complex padlock system and then pushing open the very wide gate, driving the vehicle through, closing the gate, and then relocking the gate and getting back into the vehicle took at best 4 to 6 minutes on a night without wind.

(4) Aymerich/Olmos **questioned Roofus recorded time data by, they claim, taking star readings to discover that my "uncontrolled" Roofus time reference was in error.** I opened the door to this by using the term "uncontrolled clock," meaning that the clock was not equipped to automatically synchronize with a universal time signal. Yes, the clock might have been in error by some number of seconds or even a minute or two because electric power at the ranch house (the power source for Roofus) had occasional hiccups during lightning storms and "wrist-watch time" was probably used to reset. A small error in stated time-of-day, however, is irrelevant in this case, since the only time factor required to plot ML routes was Roofus **elapsed time**, which is something they should have realized. **Most importantly, there was no indication that the clock itself was failing to function properly; elapsed time was in no way compromised**.

| Example #2 | **Camera shake? Mirage/looming? May 8, 2003** |

My photograph below shows this ML in a climbing trajectory, rising an estimated 80 to 90 meters above local terrain and then exploding (See **Strange Lights,** pp. 90-94.) The ML light track includes a significant "off-state"; it seemed to become invisible for a brief time, creating a gap in the light track. It then resumed illumination, still on track, both in time and direction. (These temporary ML-off states were a common ML characteristic. A possible explanation for this behavior is discussed in Chapter 7, not reviewed by Aymerich/Olmos).

Figure 4. Exploding ML on May 8, 2003 (Fig. 28 in Strange Lights).

The photograph's most revealing feature is the **explosive ending** that shows material raining down, in a sloping trajectory indicative of mass and momentum (see image above). How did Aymerich/Olmos explain this photograph as a truck driving on a ranch road? They contend that atmospheric looming and "camera shake" account for the climbing trajectory and explosive end. I disagree with both conclusions for multiple reasons. First, their "camera shake" explanation is inconsistent with individual falling elements that are clearly visible in Figure 4 above. Camera shake during a time exposure would drag the image out of line, but still retain the image; it would not skip from point to point. There should be a continuous excursion of the image during a camera shake. The image of this explosive event shows individual elements of falling debris moving forward in a downward-sloping trajectory, indicative of mass and momentum. **This image is very much inconsistent with their claim of vehicle headlights**. Why would they

32

expect anyone to believe their claim that this image was generated by headlights? Does this image look anything like headlights? I certainly don't think it does.

This image is also inconsistent with their claim of "looming" because obvious evidence of falling remnants indicate that this event was in the air. I estimate that it was about 80 to 90 meters in the air.

As standard procedure, my tripod cameras were always firmly grounded; I routinely used weights to guard against intermittent gusts of wind, but simply stopped filming when the wind was too strong. **I would have known, discounted and discarded this image, if the camera had been bumped.** As to the second point, the "looming" explanation, **I was there, taking these photographs**. I would have noted mirage conditions if there had been any and would have discounted this image. Their VHL-looming claim should be discounted if for no other reason than the procedure these two fellows went through to put this light on a road. A quick summary of their "analysis" provides in painful detail a good example of how this team worked:

Aymerich/Olmos used nine pages and thirteen pictures and illustrations to make their case that this was only a looming VHL (Aymerich/Olmos, pp.49-58). Most bizarre was their effort to select a suitable road from which to loom. They labeled road segments in the general area as **o & m, n & k, and h & g as pairs** to be considered. They discarded **n & k** because headlights on these two segments would be displaced in opposite directions. They admitted that segments **h & g** also had drawbacks. That left them with road segments **o & m**, a curving road that descends from the mesas running in a roughly NE direction to reach Escondido Ranch. This is an amazing choice, given that this ML was so obviously following a climbing trajectory to the NW (not NE) while traveling in a relatively straight (not curving) line. They show these road segment pairs on their pages 51 and 52; this is in an area roughly 2600 meters by 3900 meters. This is one example of how far they have reached in a virtually unlimited attempt to relocate my photographs down and over in search of a road. And this is their scientific proof that this light is a VHL? Here is a quick comparison of findings:

	Trajectory	Direction	Ending
Bunnell	*climbing* straight line	*NW*	*exploding* falling debris
A/O	*descending* curved path	*SE*	*camera bump*

Please look again at my picture of this event. You be the judge. If you had watched it, would you rely on Google Earth, using terrain data from many years after the event, to tell you whether this light, not visible in Google Earth, was ascending or descending? Moving right or moving left? No? Well, neither did I. Moreover, rancher Kerr Mitchell, witnessed this event **in the sky** from his house, more than ten miles away. He said it was the biggest ML event he had ever seen. His view from his ranch home was 90 degrees from my view at the MLVP and is inconsistent with their mirage/looming claim. Their "story" for this ML is further evidence that the Aymerich/Olmos work is not a scientific effort; I contend it is a massive misuse of technology in a failed attempt to convince readers that the Marfa Lights phenomenon does not exist.

Example #3	**VHL Electric filaments vs combustion, February 19, 2003**

Is it possible to tell the difference between the light that comes from a campfire and the light emitted from an electrified metallic filament in the headlight of a vehicle? Yes, of course. Both emit photons but they are fundamentally different light sources. Headlights are electric powered photon generators that emit smooth, uniform light, mostly in one direction; they use reflector cones to assist in concentrating emitted light in an intended direction. Fires also emit photons, but as a direct product of fuel oxidation, involving combustion of gas, liquid, or solids. **These different light sources do not look the**

34

same when viewed up close. This was the case with an ML I photographed on February 19, 2003 (**Strange Lights**, pp.74-79).

This remarkably clear ML event, shown in Figures 6-8 below, appears on the cover and pages 75-76 (Figures 19-21) of my **Strange Lights** book. I estimated that this ML was less than 1 km from my location, flying east to west at an altitude of 3 to 5 meters. These three close images show what I believe is unmistakable evidence of **an ongoing combustion process** in contrast to smooth uniform light emitted by vehicle headlights. Figure 5 shows the ML passing nearby directly in front of me, left to right. The image shows a beautifully detailed pattern of **combustive activity** captured by my tripod-mounted Canon film camera. This first image ends in a bright ball of light.

Expecting that it might reappear and continue its journey west (turning on, off, and then back on is typical ML behavior), I quickly repositioned the camera, anticipating that the ML would restart, and again pushed the remote shutter release. Almost immediately, the ML reappeared in another bright ball of light and continued its journey west. After watching it travel beyond my camera's field of view, I again repositioned the camera and managed to capture a third and final picture that reveals fascinating evidence of a decaying combustion pattern as the ML continued west, expending energy. It went out before I could capture a fourth image. The final image, Figure 8, is enlarged slightly to better show details of how the combustive process is slowing and fading.

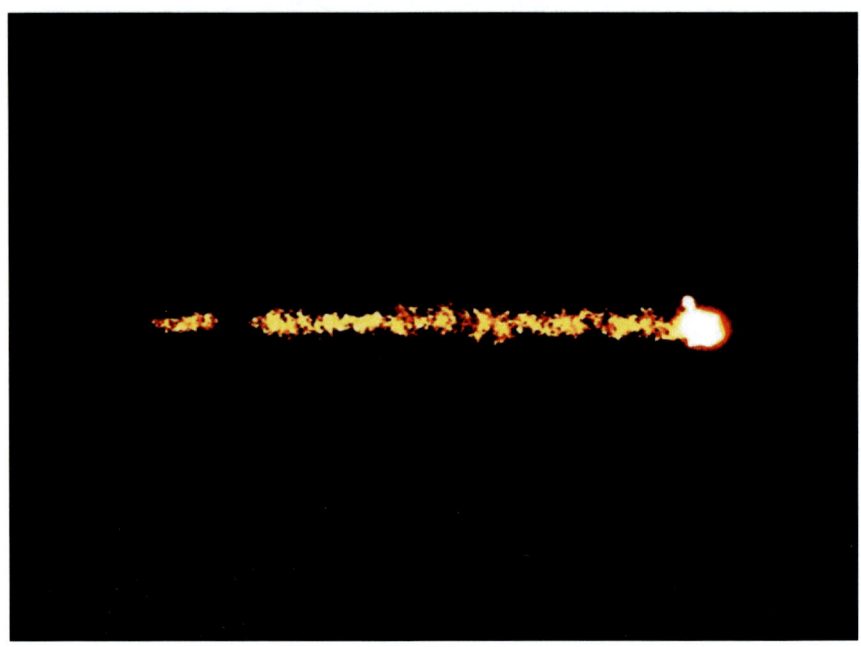

Figure 5. First (#1) 2003 ML light track (Fig. 19 in Strange

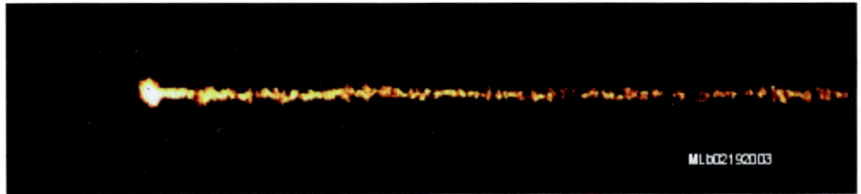

Figure 6. Second (#2) 2003 ML light track (Fig. 20 in Strange Lights).

Figure 7. Third (#3) 2003 ML light track (Fig. 21 in Strange lights).

Aymerich/Olmos (Appendix 2: Comments on Bunnell's Response) deemed this series of images to be a ranch truck driving west 10 kilometers away on Nopal Road. Because my photographs do not look anything like pictures of vehicle headlights, I challenged Olmos to photograph passing vehicles at night and show a comparison **at the scale of images presented in my book**. Their response was to produce their Figure 91, the reduced-size composite photograph shown below:

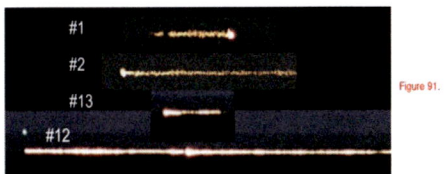

Figure 8. Aymerich/Olmos' Fig. 91 showing a reduced-size composite of four of my photographs.

Being unwilling to actually photograph passing car lights themselves (citing a variety of reasons and hindrances) Aymerich/Olmos chose to go back to an earlier book of mine, **Night Orbs**, and employ more of my photographs for comparison. I am assuming they thought this was a clever thing to do since, for them, all of my photographs are vehicle headlights. I believe they knew they had zero chance of finding vehicle headlights that would look even remotely like these 2003 close-encounter ML photographs. They intentionally reduced the size of my photographs for the comparison, I think, to make the internal composition aspects of both sets less obvious and therefore less chance of appearing mysterious. They then took seven pages of their book to create a contorted explanation of why these were VHLs, not MLs. In short, they completely failed my challenge.

Photographs #1, #2, #13, and #12 (in Fig.9 above) are all MLs. I estimated light tracks #1 and #2 to be less than 1 km (approximately half a mile) away from my camera. I had photographed light tracks #12 and #13 in May 2003. From, by my estimate, they were located more than more than 10km (6+ miles) away from my position at the MLVP. The differences between the two sets of photos are created by difference in distance from the camera, and, I believe, the extent to which #1 and #2 reveal ongoing, but waning, combustive events. Notice that the #2 light track (the larger #2, aka Figure 7, provides the better view) is getting thinner, more stretched out, and is becoming less bright as it continues beyond my location. **I believe that Aymerich/ Olmos omitted my #3 light track completely because it is especially difficult to characterize this ML as a VHL.** It appears to be losing energy, getting noticeably darker, and the between-burst spacing is becoming more elongated on its way to complete energy exhaustion. Before I could take another picture, it did go out completely.

Vehicles of people who live and work in Mitchell Flat can be seen from the MLVP driving on Nopal road on their way to or from Marfa or Alpine. During many hours onsite with my tripod mounted cameras, I observed such vehicles many times and became very familiar with Nopal traffic. Light track #1 was chosen for the cover of **Strange Lights** because it was unique in my set of ML photographs and so **very much different from vehicle traffic on Nopal Road**. It clearly shows an ongoing combustion process (as do all three of my 2/19/2003 photographs) that is not at all characteristic of VHLs.

Had this been a vehicle, it was close enough for me to easily hear vehicle sounds from its engine and off-road grinding and bouncing through desert brush and tumble weeds. But there were no sounds to be heard. I should also have been able to clearly see taillights as it passed directly in front of me, left to right. As my photographs show, there were no taillights and no vehicle. It was instead a most interesting and revealing ML.

Example #4   **The road does not fit, you must admit! May 8, 2004**

My photograph of this ML (below) is shown twice in Figure 10, once in the top frame (a very dark background version of my Figure 33 in **Strange Lights**) and overlayed onto Google Earth terrain in the frame below it. These two frames appear in Aymerich/Olmos' Figure 75. Not included here is a third, bottom frame that shows just the Google Earth terrain without the ML.

Figure 9. This light appears as Fig. 33 in Strange Lights and Fig. 75 in Aymerich/Olmos.

The above images are from Aymerich/Olmos composite Figure 75 (see Aymerich/Olmos, pp. 96-103). The top image is **ML3c** (5/8/2004), extracted without permission from my Figure 33, page 98, in *Strange Lights* (pp. 96-101). The lower image is their attempt to show a clear picture of the terrain using Google Earth, with colored lines added, to show where they say local roads were located [Note: dirt roads are clearly visible in Google Earth without need for colored lines to further shape them.] The lower image above (it is the middle image in their composite figure) is intended to show the light that my camera captured in 2004 pasted against Google terrain. **Notice how this photo-overlay relocation puts some of the light on the side of a sheer bluff.** I presume it was, on occasion, just especially difficult to find a suitable road to use. Aymerich/Olmos attempt to explain this "bright spot" and related differences with four more Google Earth maps as well as a couple of pages of text. The roads they suggest as being a possible source of this bluff-side circle of light are identified in their Figure 77 as being **w**, **v**, **u**, or **p.** Once again, they are not shy about searching far and wide for available roads. In this case they say, "road section **v**" is probably the best possibility. Let me be clear: "probably best choice" is not proof of ANYTHING. But this one requires more than "road shopping"; it comes with a fancy narrative.

Here is an amazing slice of their thinking on that road choice, i.e., what it took to put my light on a mesa road (Aymerich/Olmos, ~pp.100-101). **If you will read all of this passage, I believe you will understand why I say these two people have simply taken Google Earth and Bunnell data and molded them into the conclusions they so clearly want.**

"Possibility 2) The vehicle drove by road section S, but not by section Q, linking with P through R. At first sight it might seem an impossible combination, but there is a way out. As Figure 78 shows, the driver of the vehicle could have missed the detour where section r begins (just after section t), going through section s before realizing the error. <u>To retrace his steps, he could have traversed back just about 75m through section s, to deviate later by section r</u> and continue his way through road section p. <u>If the correction maneuver were carried out backwards,</u> the vehicle headlights would have continued pointing in the general direction of the camera, which would explain why the intensification of the photographed luminous trace extends to the right beyond direction R. <u>That is, the headlights would have been recorded twice passing through section s,</u> first moving to the right and then to the left, maybe at a lower speed if the vehicle was moving in reverse (incidentally, a lower speed would contribute to a higher intensity of the luminous track in the photograph). In short, <u>this option is not as far-fetched as it might appear</u> at first sight and, in fact, may well turn out to be the most likely solution." [p.100, Aymerich/ Olmos, The Marfa Lights...; 2020]

And all of this (I have underlined the highlights) was done to explain a set of pictures that showed not one trace of the body of an actual vehicle! In addition, there is a second elephant in the room: all of those road sections are located on top of the mesa and that means their light beams could not have been aligned to put a circle of light on the bluff-side that is located at a lower altitude out of sight from any of those road segments. In addition, the road directions they selected are misaligned with the bright spot location on the bluff below.

40

```
┌ ─ ─ ─ ─ ─ ─ ─ ─ ─ ─ ─ ─ ┐
│  Example #5             │
│                         │
└ ─ ─ ─ ─ ─ ─ ─ ─ ─ ─ ─ ─ ┘
```

**Extraordinary ML activity
on top of fault line,
October 19, 2006**

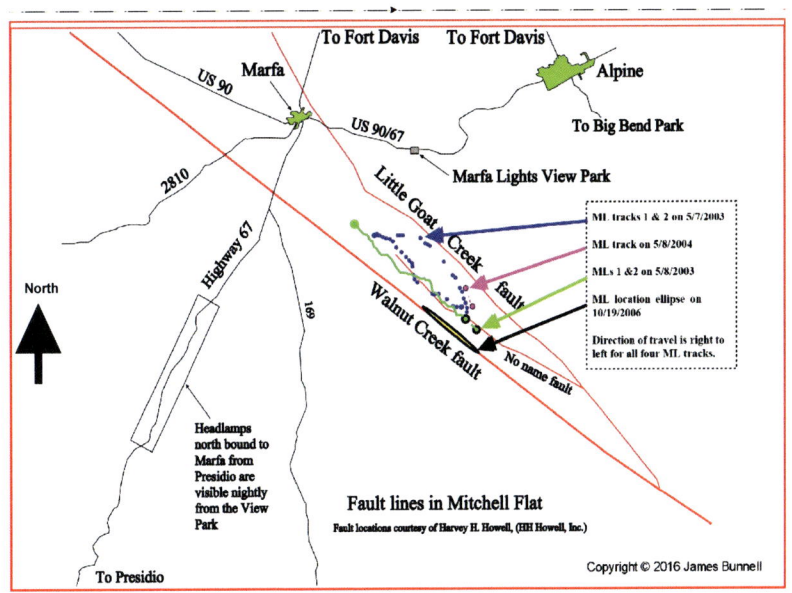

Figure 10. *Location of some MLs with respect
to fault lines in Mitchell Flat.*

In researching their confusing presentation, I also discovered that road segment "w" does a steep climb to reach the mesa top at a bearing of 158.8 degrees true from my location at the MLVP SW

41

Plaque instead of 159.1 degrees as they show in Figures 69, 71, and 75. How many other "true" vector errors might be found in their lengthy debunk document? [Note: Examples 3 & 4 above include one Aymerich/Olmos generated figure each. My copyrighted photographs, reproduced in their book without permission, are central to both of their figures, a fact that renders invalid any claim they might make that I have violated their copyright.]

My October 2006, photographs captured ML events that moved northwest on top of the Walnut Creek fault line. In general, ML flights that I was able to discover tended to travel northwest pretty much parallel to existing fault lines. As a child, I can remember some of them being seen northwest of Marfa in line with what I now know to be the Little Goat Creek fault line that extends in that direction beyond Marfa. Figure 11 shows the relationship between some ML locations and fault lines in Mitchell Flat (**Strange Lights**, pp.108-121).

Aymerich/Olmos attempted to explain away ML images collected 10/19/2006, as being caused by a defect in my lens. Their claim is inconsistent with the changing pattern of images in this collection of sequential time exposures. These ML photographs appear in this book as Figures 12-17. They appear in **Strange Lights** (pp. 110-115) as composite Figures 38-43; these include 42 separate images displaying this incredible ML light event in detail. The ML was located on top of the Walnut Creek fault as shown in the above map. It advanced NW following the fault line. My camera that night was a Canon 300D DSLR modified to enable collection of infrared frequencies. Thanks to this modification, the camera was able to capture heated air that appears in these images as "red matter" trailing behind as the ML continues flying northwest into a 10 to 7-mph headwind based on weather data for that night (**Hunting Marfa Lights,** p. 275).

Figure 11. From Strange Lights, Image 397, Figure 39, page 111.

Any careful examination of these images shows what looks like "legs" coming first from the bottom of the ML and trailing behind the advancing ML.

As these "legs" cool in the night air, my many images show a sequence of elongation and fading with increasing separation from the advancing ML. They trail behind the ML with increasing distance, fading, and finally extinguishing. The advancing ML releases a second mass of heated air that is similar in appearance but, this time, the legs detach from the top of the advancing ML instead of from the bottom. Do these images look like vehicle headlights?

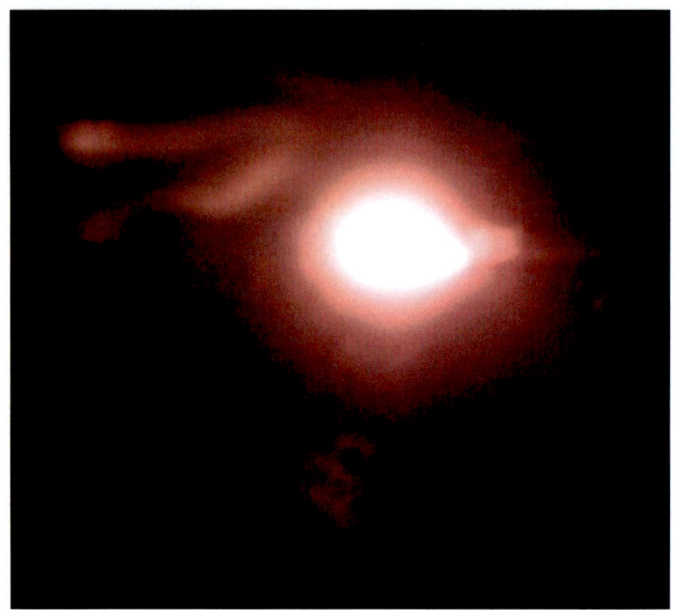

Figure 12. From *Strange Lights*, Figure 412, p113, p113.

Figure 13. From *Strange Lights*, Figure 46, page 121.

Five of the 42 images are shown here plus five on the cover of this book. All of them are included in my **Strange Lights in West Texas** book for anyone who finds these displays as interesting as I do.

My question: How could a lens defect cause what appears in this series of changing images? First, we see "leg-like" features that detach from the bottom of the advancing ML. Then, in this continuous photo collection, we see a second set of similar features detach from the top. I used that camera-telescope combination many times and there has never been any hint of a lens defect. Perhaps they were speculating that these images might be "Cassegrain Ghosts". Cassegrain Ghosts are rare aberrations that can sometimes (rarely) occur at extreme angles because of curvature in the main mirror. Ghost aberration would not even begin to explain these photographs because the "so called legs" streamed first from the bottom and then, with no camera movement, a second set appeared to detach from the top. <u>In both cases, they became elongated and faded as they trailed behind the ML, losing energy, fading, and finally going out.</u> They were neither lens aberrations nor lens defects .

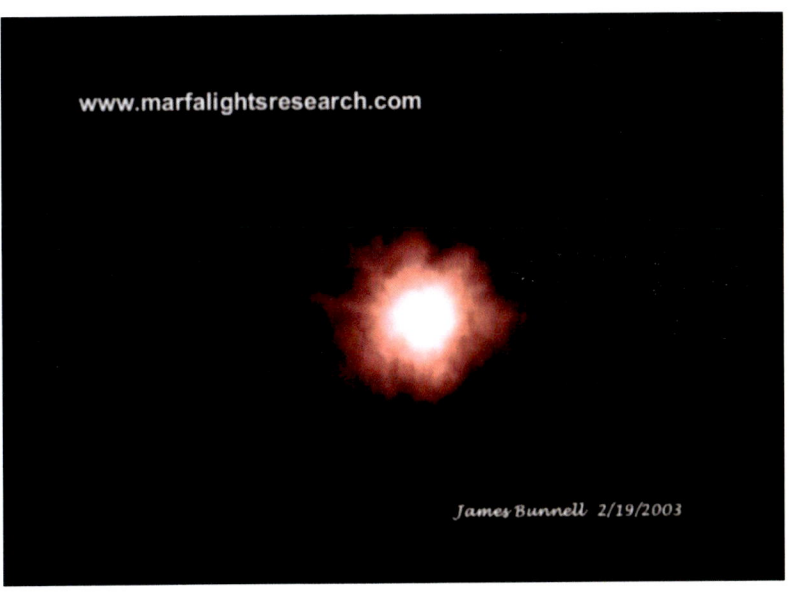

Figure 14. *From Strange Lights, Fig. 50, image 683, p127.*

While I was busy tracking these lights with an infrared capable camera, my wife, Sandra Dees, was also observing them using a

refractor (non-Cassegrain) telescope with greater magnification but no camera. She expressed amazement at what she was seeing, reporting that "The center of the ML looked like **a ball of active flames**." This magnified internal action that she was seeing was not captured with any of my modified-for-infrared camera's photographs; these show only very bright, white centers.

Please take another look at the ML photographs in Figures 11-15. I believe they show MLs expending energy and decomposing. They travel through the air for a time and then go out completely.

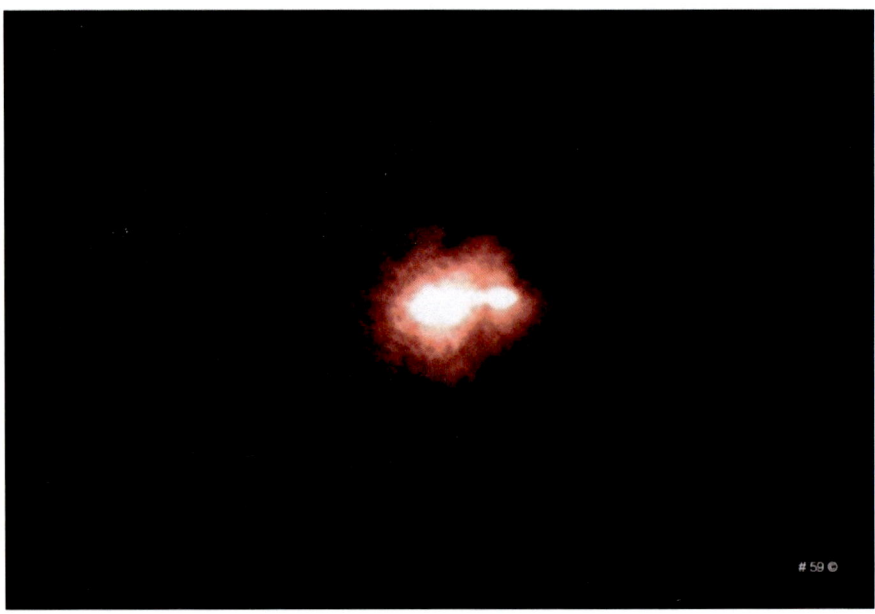

Figure 15. From Strange Lights, Fig. 50, image 682, p.127.

As an engineer I kept looking for the source of energy necessary to sustain these energetic displays. ML durations in my experience varied anywhere from milliseconds to hours but most were between 1 and 10 minutes (median = 4 minutes from 52 events). Photographic evidence shows that MLs are consuming energy as clearly shown in Example 3, Figures 6-8, and the above photographs. They consume

46

energy and then they go out. Headlights, in contrast, provide uniform energy profiles and, if they are working normally, they do not go out. **So, there are significant, measurable differences between VHLs and MLs that were being captured by my digital cameras.**

I operated my cameras in a mode that automatically adjusted exposure times based on light intensity. This camera feature was necessary to obtain best quality photographs, especially in dark conditions. This camera capability not only produced better images, but it also provided direct evidence of variability in ML light intensity as shown in Figure 17 below.

What did the energy consumption rates look like for separate images in this set of pictures? One way to gain some insight is to plot camera-selected exposure times as shown in Figure 17. The first five ML images are displayed on the cover of this response.

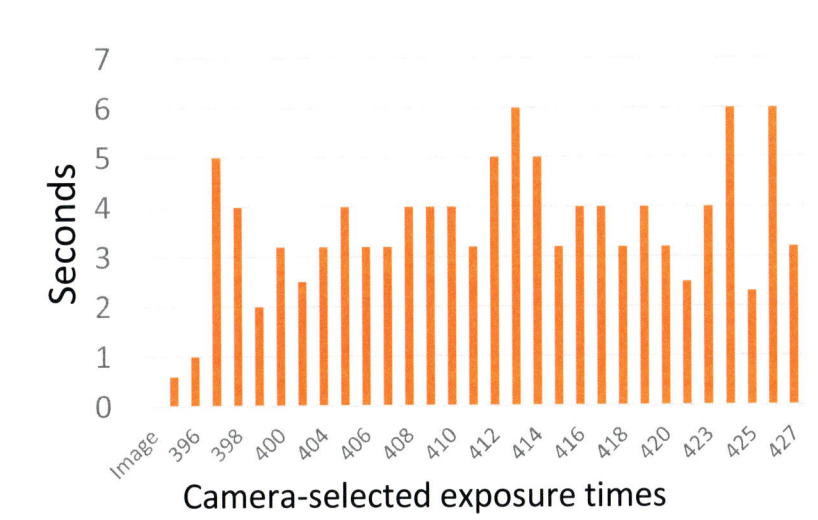

Figure 16. Thirty camera-selected exposure times show evidence of wide variability in ML intensity (ML: 10/19/2006, Figs. 12-16). This stands in contrast to the uniform energy that would be expected with a comparable VHL display.

There is always much to consider in ML studies, but for the purpose of this response, I ask readers to consider the fact that these camera selected exposures times are inconsistent with uniform vehicle head light displays. In addition, I suggest this shows light variability, not a lens defect. The fact that Sandra Dees was also witness to this night's ML light variability, using a refractor telescope with significant magnification (easily capable of detecting vehicles; something she wanted to ensure that we were not unintentionally photographing headlights), reinforces this claim. Instead of an approaching vehicle, she was seeing "intense orange-red flame-like activity" in the centers of these displays.

This October 2006, sequence of photographs may be among the most revealing and valuable ML captures recorded during my investigation. To the best of my knowledge, science still does not have a clear understanding of exactly how positive and negative plasma ions orbit, but the unusual capture of these bottom and top leg-like heated air discharges may offer interesting clues. This kind of photography, and the questions it raises, are just one of many reasons why earth lights need serious scientific investigation. My photographic evidence shows that unlike smooth electric headlights, MLs are balls of energy that are being consumed by the displays they produce. I suspect that the core ML energy source is plasma but that the visible light we see, and that I was photographing, are conventional hydrogen/oxygen fires resulting from ongoing state conversions as the core plasma is cooling in the night air. This would also explain why MLs display spectra are typical of combustion fires instead of plasma. How is it possible that these Strange Lights are able to fly into the wind? There has to be more to this story than what I was able to discover during my limited effort. To dismiss these phenomena based on shallow pseudoscience from the other side of the world is a mistake.

A final note

I have shown you, and readers of my books, what I consider to be evidence of Marfa's mysterious lights and my tentative conclusions regarding the significance of that data. More discussion/speculation is available in Chapter 9 of **Strange Lights**. The only thing Aymerich and Olmos have shown you is their ability to use Google Earth, looking far and wide, to find roads where VHLs might have traveled. When you get into the "weeds" of what they have done, you will find that both their use of Google Earth and their conclusions are based on heavily biased opinion and unsupported assumptions.

Scientists currently are researching "earth lights" in countries such as Norway, Italy, South America, and Australia. They were doing this long before my limited effort near Marfa, and will continue, I hope, until scientific investigations finally reveal the source and nature of what I believe to be natural phenomena, very real and, in my humble opinion, well deserving of government and university research support. I was fortunate enough in retirement to be able to fund my own efforts, but even so, I worked alone and would have welcomed a university team with cameras. Aymerich/Olmos could not have done their "research" without my hard work and expense, and without the unethical and illegal use of a myriad of copyrighted materials from my books and websites.

It would be wrong to take Aymerich/Olmos as the last word on earth lights. Their work shows a relentless determination -- a huge bias -- to find a single predetermined, and, in this case unnatural (headlights) explanation for MLs. It saddens me that their work will likely reduce scientific interest in earth lights, making acquisition of research support more difficult. I sincerely hope that some voices in the scientific community will speak out about the need for such research, debunkers notwithstanding.

What do I think today about light phenomena that sometimes (albeit rarely) displays above Mitchell Flat and other worldwide locations? I believe Earth Lights are an untapped science goldmine that may, one day, contribute to a deeper understanding of atomic forces. Our modern civilization is the product of man's advancement in understanding science, but to assume we now know everything is a mistake. These fellows from Spain are bright people. They could be using their talents to advance science instead of bashing fledgling research efforts of others. A positive contribution would have served them <u>much</u> better.

Certainly, there is more that could be said in support of Mysterious Marfa Lights, but this summary says enough. **Hunting Marfa Lights** and this book are available as eBooks via internet sources.

Part 3

Night camera sites "Roofus," "Snoopy," & "Owlbert"
** Examples of my mobile cameras.

Figure 17. Roofus, my first automated night camera site.

This camera was located on Kerr Mitchell's ranch at the western end of Mitchell Flat. It had a clear view of the Central Mercury Vapor Lamp (CMV), a light that provided a fixed, directional reference. The CMV was located south and east of Roofus, near the middle of Mitchell Flat on Barlight Ranch. It was important to my calculations enabling travel route tracking for some MLs. The CMV ceased to function eventually ceased functioning and has not been replaced by ranch owners.

Figure 18. View from Roofus showing, left to right, Goat Mountain, a UL (unidentified light), and the CMV. This view is typical.

Night camera video data was recorded every night on removable hard drives. At the end of each trip to Marfa, I replaced those drives with reformatted drives and took the loaded drives to my home office for detailed data reviews. This ongoing continuous review of data from hard drives allowed me to assess, from other vantage points, light activity I had photographed during my visit, and to gain insight as well into the frequency and variability of nightly ground and airborne light traffic. Along with MLs, my cameras recorded many interesting night sky phenomena including many Sprites and, in one incredibly rare case, a Giant Jet.

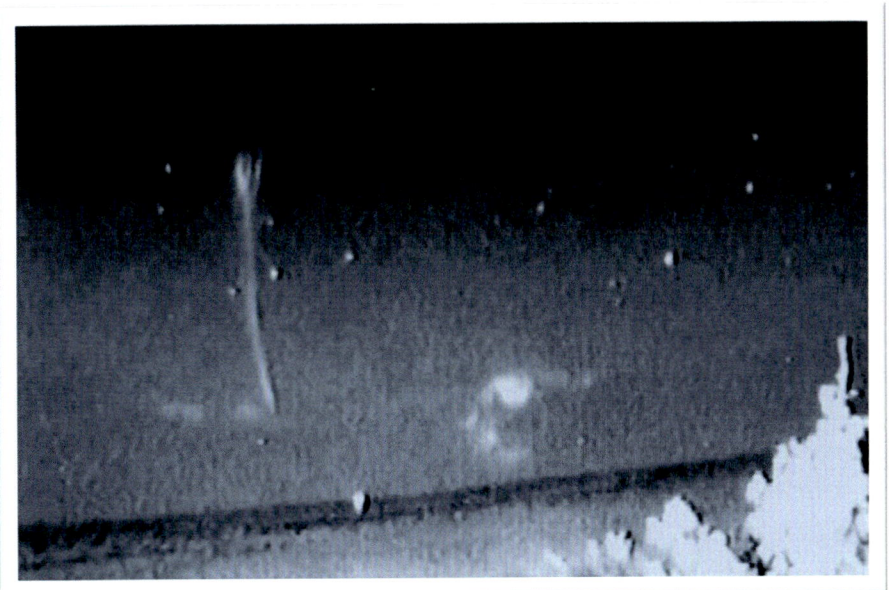

Figure 19. The stalk-like figure is a Giant Jet recorded by Roofus (it was also clearly captured by Snoopy) on May 13, 2005.

The two photographs I have (the Snoopy shot was not included here) were, and, so far as I know, still are, the only photographs ever taken of a giant jet above the North American Continent. It was located approximately 200 miles away over Mexico, south of Del Rio, Texas. The splitting at the top is where the upward stream of ions exited the earth's atmosphere. The event lasted 80 milliseconds. [Sprites are ions being pulled down out of the Van Allen belts (my night cameras captured many Sprites from storms over the horizon. Extremely rare Giant jets are ion streams going the other way, up into Van Allen belts.] This photograph is testimony to the capability of my night cameras to do what they were intended to do: photograph lights, specifically lights of unknown origin (MLs). This giant jet event was reported in the Journal of Geophysical Research, 2007 (van der Velde, Lyons, Nelson, Cunner, Li, Bunnell).

Snoopy

Snoop with two cameras

OCT 9 21

Figure 20. Snoopy Power Station.

The night camera site, "Snoopy," (shown above) was located on a hill approximately 3 miles SE from Roofus. It became operational in 2004 and generated its own electric power. The night image below, from Snoopy, clearly shows Goat Mountain and the Barlight Central Mercury Vapor (CMV), two known points that anchored lights tracked by both Roofus and Snoopy, allowing me to calculate detailed ML routes across Mitchell Flat. Snoopy had one camera in the beginning, but I later added a second camera.

Figure 21. The view from Snoopy, with the CMV light visible to the right of Goat Mountain.

Owlbert

In 2006, thanks to two wonderful ranch owners, I was able to add seven more cameras centrally located in two stations (Owlbert A & B shown below). The addition of these seven cameras significantly enhanced ML acquisition and confirmation capabilities. Being able to match individual camera frames from different recorders required precise time control. To meet that need, I started pulling time data from satellites for all ten cameras.

Figure 22
Owlbert Night Cameras
The top image shows night station Owlbert A equipped with four cameras. The bottom image was station Owlbert B equipped with three cameras. The recorder was multichannel with hard drives. The addition of these seven cameras in 2006 provided wider coverage of Mitchell

Two Examples of My Mobile Camera Setups

Figure 26.

Figure 27.

References

Aymerich, B. M., & Olmos, V. J. B. (2020). *The Marfa Lights, Examining the Photographic Evidence (2003 – 2007)*. Barcelona, Spain: [Internet Publication].

Brueske, J. M. (1989). *The Marfa Lights*. Alpine, Texas: Ocotillo Enterprises.

Bunnell, J. (2003). *Night Orbs*. Cedar Creek, Texas: Lacey Publishing Company.

Bunnell, J. (2009). *Hunting Marfa Lights*. Benbrook, Texas: Lacey Publishing Company.

Bunnell, J. (2015). *Strange Lights in West Texas*. Benbrook, Texas: Lacey Publishing Company.

Freund, F. T., Takeuchi, A., & Lau, B. W. S. (*2006). Electrical currents streaming out of stressed igneous rocks---A step towards understanding pre-earthquake low frequency EM emissions*. *Journal of Physics and Chemistry of the Earth, 31*.

McGookey, D.P. (2004). **Geologic Wonders of West Texas.** Midland, Texas:

Stephan, K.D., Bunnell, J., Klier, J., & Komala-Noor, L. (2011). *Quantitative intensity and location measurements of an intense long-duration luminous object near Marfa, Texas. Journal of Atmospheric and Solar-Terrestrial Physics, 73, No. 13*.

Teodorani, M. (*2004). A long-term scientific survey of the Hessdalen phenomenon, Journal of Scientific Exploration, 18, No.2*.

van der Velde, O. A., Lyons, W. A., Nelson, T. E., Cummer, S. A., Li, J. & Bunnell, J. (*2007). Analysis of the first giant jet recorded over continental North America. Journal of Geophysical Research, 11*.

Wagers, R. & Wagers (2013). **Mysteries of the Marfa Lights Revealed,** RJ Books Unique, Richardson, Texas.

James Bunnell, Marfa, Texas. 2009.

In the search for truth, I experimented with many different approaches, configurations, and equipment combinations. It wasn't quite as simple as using someone else's work.

I am extremely grateful to Kerr and Mary Belle Mitchell (dear friends, now deceased), Richard and Robert Nunley, owners of Barlight Ranch, Marfa-based ranch people, my loving spouse Dr.Sandra Dees, my brother Will and Dr. Karl Stephan, all of whom assisted me in countless ways, enabling and making possible my decade-long research effort.

My work ended with the publication of **Strange Lights in West Texas** in 2015. For me, this quest was happily finished with that book. But I could not remain completely silent in the face of this outlandish effort to bury the Marfa Lights -- Texas earth lights, an untapped natural treasure.